Thrive

Co-Written by
Trina Olson & *Tina Hoover*

© Copyright 2024 – Radical Launch International Ministries
All rights reserved. This book is protected by the copyright laws of the United States of America. This book may not be copied or reprinted for commercial gain or profit. The use of short quotations or occasional page copying for personal use is permitted and encouraged. Permission will be granted upon request.

Unleashed Publishing, Inc.
947 Wayne Avenue #351
Chambersburg, Pa 17201
We can be reached by calling (717) 860-1848 or through our Website:
unleashedpublishing.net

ISBN-13: 978-1-7356913-4-3
ISBN-10: 1-7356913-4-3

Table of Contents

Friday Night Session …...9
Note Section..12
Questions for the activation. 14
What was it like when you had a baby? 17
Saturday Session…..19
How to practice his presence?..............................21
Love Wins..22
Be Kind …..23
Keep it Simple & Smile ….....................................24
Keep Your Bible Open …......................................25
What is Your Story? …...29
Why Encounters Matter …....................................33

How can we have the right to encounter the Lord?............35

What does the scripture say about encounters?...................37

Jesus Empowered the Woman at the Well 51

Closing the Doors of our Past.................................57

The Power of our Testimony..................................61

The Transformation of Zacchaeus...........................63

How to reverse the plans of the enemy?..............................67
Redefining a fact you have been believing all your life....*69*
References. 71

"Thrive"

Friday Night Session
Finding His Goodness in the Hard

Notes Sections:

Together is Enough

_____
_____
_____
_____
_____

Training our Eyes

_____
_____
_____
_____
_____

He doesn't do abandonment

Pain demands attention

Inviting Him Inside

Questions for the activation:

1. Ask Jesus to take you back to an important event in your life.

   _____
   _____
   _____
   _____

2. Ask Him what is significant about this event?

   _____
   _____
   _____
   _____

3. What emotions do you feel as you remember what happened?

   _____
   _____
   _____
   _____

4. Ask Jesus to show you the lie that you believed.

5. Ask Jesus to show you where that lie came from (the root).

6. Ask Jesus to reveal the truth to you.

7. Confess to Jesus that you have believed the lie.

8. Ask the Holy Spirit to heal the wound.

9. Declare the truth over yourself.

What was it like when you had a baby?

Remember the attachment you had with your child? As your child cried, you met the need. A baby learns attachment and trust by 2+ years old. In a healthy environment the trust is not destroyed during a crisis moment and their identity is not affected. Our parenting reflects the Father.

Saturday Sessions

Finally, brethren, whatever things are true, whatever things are noble, whatever things are just, whatever things are pure, whatever things are lovely, whatever things are of good report, if there is any virtue and if there is anything praiseworthy—meditate on these things. Philipeans4:8 (NKJV)

_____

_____

_____

_____

_____

_____

_____

_____

_____

_____

_____

_____

_____

_____

_____

_____

_____

_____

How to practice his presence?

Love Wins
It is the Only Way!

Love suffers long *and* is kind; love does not envy; love does not parade itself, is not puffed up, does not behave rudely, does not seek its own, is not provoked, thinks no evil; does not rejoice in iniquity, but rejoices in the truth; bears all things, believes all things, hopes all things, endures all things. Love never fails. But whether *there are* prophecies, they will fail; whether *there are* tongues, they will cease; whether *there is* knowledge, it will vanish away. 1 Corinthians 13:4-8 (NKJV)

And above all things have fervent love for one another, for "love will cover a multitude of sins." 1 Peter 4:8 (NKJV)

We love Him because He first loved us. 1 John 4:19 (NKJV)

Let love *be* without hypocrisy. Abhor what is evil. Cling to what is good. Romans 12:9 (NKJV)

Beloved, let us love one another, for love is of God; and everyone who loves is born of God and knows God. 1 John 4-7 (NKJV)

Be Kind

"When you are good to others, we are best to yourself."
Ben Franklin

And be kind to one another, tenderhearted, forgiving one another, even as God in Christ forgave you. Ephesians 4:32 (NKJV)

Keep it Simple & Smile

"We shall never know all the good that a simple smile can do."
"One filled with joy preaches without preaching"
Mother Teresa

Keep Your Bible Open

"I will study and prepare myself, and someday my chance will come."
"Whatever you are, be a good one."
Abraham Lincoln

You Got This!

Your Story is Beautiful

He is in the Details

His Worship is Key

Restoration – Newness - Go get all He has for you.

What is Your Story?

Why Encounters Matter

Why is it important to have God encounters and what are encounters?

An encounter is a meeting with the Lord that can happen in many different ways. You can encounter the Lord through dreams or visions, during worship, through prayer, or simply sitting in silence. When you encounter the Lord, it may be the Father, Jesus, the Holy Spirit, an angel of the Lord, or even through other heavenly beings. Usually when you have a significant encounter your life will be forever changed.

Encounters are not just an outward manifestation but can be a gentle nudge of the Holy Spirit; it could be a whisper of correction or a moment of hearing "I love you" from the Father; it could be a deep understanding of something in your spirit that gives you an unction of direction that saves your life; maybe a deep inner healing of Jesus healing your childhood trauma or a wound of yesterday; what about a vison or a trance of the future that will give you insight to your destiny; or an encounter where the Father or Jesus walks into your moment to help you know you are not alone. Encounters can be daily and don't have to be a rare moment in time. The more you build a relationship with the Lord, the more readily they sometimes become.

How can we have the right to encounter the Lord?

Jesus talks about giving us His glory in John 17:22-23 which says that we become one with Jesus as He is one with the Father. Jesus also says that it is so the world will know that the Father sent Him and to reveal his love to us from Jesus and through us to others.

John 17:22-23 (NIV) "I have given them the glory that you gave me, that they may be one as we are one. I in them and you in me—so that they may be brought to complete unity. Then the world will know that you sent me and have loved them even as you have loved me."

We are seated in heavenly places such as in Ephesians 2:6 (NIV) "And God raised us up with Christ and seated us with him in the heavenly realms in Christ Jesus…". We are created to encounter the Lord spirit to spirit. Just like John was taken into an encounter in Revelation 1 and Revelation 4 where the Lord revealed many things for now and for the future and requested that he would write it all down.

In Revelation 1, Jesus reveals to John that it is Jesus himself holding the keys of death and Hades. He tells John not to be afraid as he reveals to John that he was dead and now he is alive for ever and ever. What if this moment was recorded to reveal that it was a fulfilling of scripture in John 21 when Jesus answers Peter's questioned how John would die? Jesus says to Peter "If I want him to remain alive until I return, what is it to you?"

In Revelation 4, the Father is revealed. Jesus, the Father, and the Holy Spirit are one with us on the throne of God. We are seated in the heavenly realm with Jesus and as we understand our position with them and that we are not them but in them, we can understand that the Lord wants to also encounter us. Jesus tells the disciples in John 14 that if you see me (Jesus) you have seen the Father.

John was a human just as we are human. He believed in Jesus and received him as his Lord and Savior. He was also baptized in the Holy Spirit which we are also able to receive. If John could have an encounter, we are also able to have encounters with the Lord. Could it be that as we understand our position with the Lord, we also will see a shift in the healing within us?

Have you ever had a heavenly encounter? How did it change your life? Is it still changing your life?

_____
_____
_____
_____
_____
_____
_____

What does the scripture say about encounters?

Let's look at several people in the Bible and how it changed their lives as they encountered either Jesus, the Father, the Holy Spirit, or even an Angel of the Lord. As you read the little snippet of information about each encounter, I challenge you to go and read those scriptures and ask God questions.

Acts 4:8-13
Peter, filled with the Holy Spirit, had a boldness and courage to confront the Jewish leaders. He boldly shares that it was Jesus whom they crucified that healed the lame man. When they saw the courage of Peter and John and realized that they were unschooled, ordinary men, they we astonished. They took note that these men had been with Jesus. Peter was forever changed. Boldness and courage came upon him and John to do what God was calling them to do.

Take Away: What would it take for you to step into your moment that God is calling you to stand in? What is holding you back from taking that step?

_____

_____

_____

_____

_____

_____

Acts 4:31
After John and Peter were released from prison, they joined up with other believers and a prayer meeting was started. As they were praying for God to enable them to speak God's word with great boldness, the meeting was shaken, and they were all filled with the Holy Spirit speaking God's word boldly.

Take Away: Has God ever shaken your foundation?

Acts 8:26-40
Philip was encountered by an angel of the Lord. The angel gave him specific directions. On his way he met an Ethiopian eunuch. The angel didn't tell him what he would do but as he went the Spirit of the Lord then directed him to go near the chariot and stay there. As he did so, he heard the man reading from the Book of Isaiah. We don't know what Philip was told by God, but we do know that Philip spoke to the man and asked him if he understood what he was reading. Philip was placed in the right place at the right time to help bring understanding. It opened a door for the gentlemen to be baptized in water and by the Spirit when suddenly the Spirit of the Lord took Philip away and the eunuch did not see him anymore. The eunuch's life was forever changed because of the obedience of Philip. The eunuch was an important official in charge of all the treasury of the Kandake (Queen of the Ethiopians). Did the life changing encounter with Philip and the Spirit of God, impact the Queen's life.

An Angel of the Lord gave him direction in an encounter. The Spirit of the Lord directed him to go near the chariot which placed in position to hear the eunuch. As Philip was obedient, he was given a word of wisdom by God to ask the Eunuch the question, "Do you understand what you are reading?" So out of his three opportunities to be obedient, God blessed three times. God gave him revelation to interpret the scriptures in Isaiah which opened a door for the Eunuch to be water baptized. As this was all happening Philip experienced the supernatural power of God as the spirit transported him to another location to preach the gospel.

Take Away: Are you willing to be obedient when it may inconvenience you? Also are you willing to go by yourself when God calls you?

Acts 9
Saul's conversion was with Jesus when he was knocked down and blinded. This was a life changing moment that changed a murderer into a devoted son of God that would change culture.

Take Away: Are we willing to not judge someone's past that God is using mightily? Are you allowing your past to limit you?

Acts 9:10

Ananias was called by God in a vision. He was able to speak in the vison and even asked God questions out of his fear. God didn't answer his questions of fear but just said "Go" and told him the importance of his mission. God sent him with a message and as Ananias laid his hands on Saul immediately scales fell from Saul's eyes, and he was healed and filled with the Holy Spirit. He then went to get water baptized. Once again, an encounter changed Ananias and gave him the ability to do what God was calling him to do. Paul was used mightily and powerfully, and his legacy is still being used to change culture today.

In this story, God had to use multiple tactics to complete the mission and to empower Ananias to step out of his comfort zone. God used Words of Knowledge to tell Ananias about Saul's location and his blindness. God also gave prophetic revelation to Ananias about Saul's future mission which was used for prophesy to speak words over Saul. Ananias was given the Spirit of Might to overcome his fear to go to Saul. The Spirit of Revelation for information about Saul's location and his future mission. Ananias had the Fear of the Lord because he knew the importance of being obedient to God. The Spirit of Understanding was also used for Ananias to understand how he was to approach Saul.

Take Away: Has God ever asked you to speak to someone that has brought fear to your heart? How did you overcome that fear?

Acts 10
Cornelius had a vison and clearly saw the angel of God. He spoke to the angel in the vision and was given specific directions to send men to bring Peter to his house. In doing so, Cornelius obedience changed an entire people group. The gentiles came to know Jesus and Holy Spirit that day. Our lives were changed because of this encounter.

Take Away: Have you ever been fearful to mingle with a person of another faith? Would you be willing to go into a Muslim community and possibly share a meal with them? Would you invite a woman of another faith to have tea or coffee with you?

Acts 10

As Peter was praying, He was taken into a trance where God showed him heaven open up. Peter also was able to speak in the encounter as he was questioning God. Peter was a Jewish man who would not eat anything unclean by their culture. It was also illegal to be with a gentile person. The angel spoke to Peter and said, "Do not call anything impure that God has made clean." That encounter changed Peter's heart toward an entire people group they were not allowed to associate with in their daily lives. As Peter was pondering the vison after coming out of it, the Spirit spoke to him about the three men looking for him. The Spirit of God spoke to Peter and said, "do not hesitate". This obedience opened the door for the Spirit of God to pour out on the gentile people just like God did for the Jewish people.

What is a Trance? (Greek G1610)- a throwing of the mind out of its normal state into a state wakefulness which his mind is drawn off from surroundings and fixed on the divine that he sees nothing but the forms and images lying within and thinks that he perceives with his bodily eyes and ears realities shown him by God.

Take away: What is God asking you to do for you to step into the next season? Would you be willing to step beyond culture or tradition to transform your culture?

Acts 12

In prison, the Angel of the Lord appears to Peter and shows him the way out. It was so powerful, Peter thought it was a vision. The angel walked with him and hid him from the guards. As they walked the large iron gates opened by itself. How radical of an encounter where God helps Peter escape from prison to rescue him from Herod's clutches.

Take away: Do you feel you are in a prison or a bondage that God could be showing you a way out off? What does your prison look like? Is it a prison of addiction? Prison of pornography? Prison of negative thoughts? Prison of illness? Fear? Anxiety? Depression? Shame?

_____
_____
_____
_____
_____
_____
_____

Are you ready to let go off this prison? Let me lead you in this exercise. Take a few slow deep breaths. Now breath in God's love. Breath in "Yah "and exhale "weh." (Yahweh a word for God). Now picture Jesus in front of you. After you get Jesus with you, hand this problem over to Jesus. Let him take away this addiction, this pain, this imprisonment. Welcome the Holy Spirit to come into this place. Picture Jesus breaking these chains.

If you feel have found victory, share your testimony of what Christ has done.

_____
_____
_____
_____
_____
_____
_____

Acts 16
The Holy Spirit prevented Paul from preaching the word in the province of Asia. Paul encountered the Spirit of Jesus which stopped them from entering Bithynia. He then was given a vision in the nighttime hours of a man of Macedonia standing and begging him to come to Macedonia to help. Paul got ready at once and headed that direction. Paul never saw the man in his vison but when he went to the river to pray, the Lord opened the heart of Lydia to respond to Paul's message. Lydia and her entire family were baptized. I believe the business world was changed in that moment also as Lydia was a dealer in purple cloth and presumed to be a very important woman in business.

Take away: How can you relate to Lydia, a woman who was a prominent businesswoman? How may God be asking you to take Him into your workplace or classroom? Do you see Jesus in the conversations that you have a work? If Jesus was standing beside you, would he be pleased with the conversation?

With each of these testimonies of the goodness of God, how has the Lord shifted your understanding of encounters with average ordinary people?

_____
_____
_____
_____
_____
_____
_____

Is there one of these Bible accounts that speaks to your heart?

___
___
___
___
___
___
___

Jesus Empowered the Woman at the Well

John Chapter 4 talks about an encounter Jesus had with the woman at the well. I would like to look at the scripture to see how Jesus ministered to her. This moment in time didn't just impact one person, it impacted an entire town through one woman having her moment with Jesus. The impact Jesus has on our lives should also impact more than just ourselves; our encounters with Jesus should also impact everyone we then encounter in our lives.

According to the scripture, Jesus was tired from his journey and sat down by a well at about noon that day. Jesus needed to find rest and, in that place, the Father brought a woman to Jesus who was in need of a life changing encounter. This was a Samaritan well, but it also belonged to the ancestors of Jacob who was a Jew. In those days, it was not lawful for a Jew to interact with a Samaritan, so why did Jesus go to that particular well? I believe the Father led Him to a divine appointment with a woman on her own journey, a woman who needed to find hope in her life or maybe she was just looking be loved for who she was.

This moment in time was so impactful that it changed the culture and made salvation available to not only the Jewish people, but also to the Samaritans. Jesus watched where the Father was and went where the Father was highlighting to him to go for his next divine appointment. He stepped away from His disciples and followed His Father. He must have done this before, because the disciples just continued on their journey without complaint. The Father has His heart set on reconciliation with His people and He was about to reconcile His daughter's heart back to Him; the Father was about to reconcile an entire generation of Samaritans back to Himself.

The woman at the well told Jesus that it was her ancestor Jacob's well. She was a descendant of Jacob, yet not considered a Jew. In God's eyes this didn't matter. In this story of the woman at the well, she was a woman by herself at the well in the heat of the middle of the day collecting water for her family. What does that say about her? That she had no friends? No one to join her on her journey? Was she an outcast who was unwanted? How many of us have been in this position at some point of our lives? Have you ever found yourself with no one to walk beside you, feeling lonely, unloved and unwanted? The Father saw her and had compassion for her and drew Jesus away from the disciples to meet with this one woman alone.

When the Samaritan Woman came to draw water, Jesus was right there waiting for her along with the Father. Jesus is right there waiting for us also in our time of need. The Samaritan woman represents someone who in their culture would have been unworthy to speak or maybe even considered an outcast. Jesus didn't bow to culture; He followed His Father in Heaven, bringing Heaven to Earth. It was not acceptable for a Jewish man to approach a Samaritan woman in that culture, but Jesus stepped across cultural limitations to allow a woman to encounter her Heavenly Father for the first time in her life. The disciples had gone on to town to buy food while Jesus was about to eat from the tree of life.

Jesus asked this woman to give Him a drink from the well. I believe she was stunned by Him asking because it was unlawful for a Jew to lower themselves by speaking to a Samaritan. Jesus' ministry was an example of how to walk out our own lifestyle of Christianity. He knew what the Father wanted to talk with her about and spoke to her in a way that was inviting, saying: "If you knew the gift of God and who it is that asks you for a drink, you would have asked him and he would have given you living water." He speaks to her in a way that causes a question in her heart: What is this living water He talks about? Who is this man? Can you imagine being that woman with Jesus sitting there asking you the same question?

I believe His eyes pierced her soul and pushed away the darkness as He spoke life into her. He spoke in a way which provoked questions. This woman was so impacted by her encounter with Jesus that her whole world changed in a moment; in a heartbeat she was forever impacted. Jesus told the woman, "Believe in Me" (John 4). Jesus then shared with the woman that a time would come (and it is now) that the worshipers would worship in spirit and truth and that they would worship neither on this mountain nor Jerusalem. He was speaking about how as we receive Jesus into our hearts, we will worship the Lord in Spirit and in truth. It is not a place, but within us where He now will reside once we accept Jesus into our hearts. We cannot get Jesus from anyone else or go to a specific place to receive Jesus. As we worship Him with all of our heart, soul, spirit, and mind, we are looking to Him as our Lord and not looking to another person to be our higher power or to be His translator for us. He alone is your living water. He alone is your salvation. In him, you will thirst no more.

The woman at the well was transformed by her encounter with Jesus. She was a new person, transformed and on a journey that would lead an entire town to Christ. This woman came to the well with a heavy heart and left with a new found life of purpose. Jesus ministered to her using the prophetic, using love, and using compassion. He never used His prophetic gifts to judge her or destroy her, but instead, He chose to give her life. Our words to other people need to give life and not death. Our words should empower others and not devalue them. This woman was so impacted by Jesus that she left her water jar behind and went back to a village that most likely hated her, filled to overflowing with a love that she poured out into each one of them while telling them what she just encountered and saying: "Could this be the Messiah?" This woman who walked in the hottest time of the day to get water by herself most likely would admit she had no friends, but the impact she made on that same town as she shared the Testimony of Jesus convinced them to drop everything, they were doing to come check out this Jesus. Do you allow the Jesus inside of you to impact others in that same way? What if we would allow Jesus to rise up inside of us to touch the community where we live?

The disciples came back and still had no ability to understand what Jesus had been doing while they had gone to get food. They were concerned for Him, thinking he needed food; however, Jesus had been fed spiritually through His encounter with the Samaritan woman. He told the disciples, "I have food to eat that you know nothing about." ... "My food, "said Jesus, "is to do the will of Him who sent me and to finish His work." Are we looking to see where the Father is highlighting for us to go next? Are you experiencing Jesus rising up inside of you every day to minister to the one in front of you? When people walk away from you, can they say they feel empowered or discouraged? Jesus' way of ministry looked different than the way we walk out ministry today and we need to take a step back and look at how Jesus ministered and apply that today in our lives.

Closing the Doors of our Past

Jesus tells us in the Bible that we are either for Him or against Him (Matthew 12:30). Jesus urges us to "follow me"! The Bible also tells us in Psalms 24:7 to "lift up you gates" to let the "King of Glory" come in. The Bible reassures us that the "gates of hell" will not prevail against us (Matthew 16:18). We are gateways, designed to release either heaven or hell depending upon whom we are serving. Before we come to know Jesus, the Lord of Glory, and make Him the Lord of our lives, we are serving the lord of darkness, satan, who rules this fallen world whether we are aware of it or not.

The Four Doors of Legal Attack

Jesus overcame the world that we also could be overcomers. Jesus overcame death that we might have life and life more abundant (John 10:10). Once we invite Jesus into our hearts we have begun to overcome the world. Jesus tells us that although we are "in the world, we are no longer of the world" (John 15:9).

However, while we were in the world we may have opened ourselves to continuing attack by satan, the enemy of our souls. There are four "doors" which we can open that give the enemy access to our lives; These doors are fear, anger, sexual promiscuity, and participation in occult activities.

When we act in fear it is because we are not trusting in God. The Bible tells us that "He did not give us a spirit of fear" (2 Timothy 1:7) but He gave us boldness and confidence and a spirit of might and a sound mind. The Bible also tells us that perfect love casts out all fear (1 John 4:18).

Anger and acting in anger is clearly not of God because Jesus tells us that if we are even angry with someone it is as if we have murdered them (Matthew 5:21-22). So when we act in anger that is clearly us choosing (whether we know it or not) to partner with satan and his ways, also known as the ways of the world. The Bible tells us that satan is the ruler of this world (Ephesians 2:2 and John 12:31) even though he actually lost all authority when Jesus went to the Cross and then descended to hell and took the keys from satan and then ascended to heaven to sit at the right hand of the Father who gave Jesus ALL Authority on earth and in Heaven (Matthew 28:18).

The next-door of legal access for satan within our lives can be opened through acts of sexual promiscuity. God made man to have one wife and enter into the covenant of holy matrimony whereby the two become one and a holy soul tie is established between the couple. When we choose to be intimate with people and have not entered into holy matrimony with them but are just involved casually, a soul tie is created that is unholy and it opens us up to attack by satan. If the one that we choose to be intimate with has been intimate with others, then we are opened up to receiving any demons which they may have collected along the way.

The fourth door of legal access for satan is opened when we participate in activities of the occult such as witchcraft, control and manipulation, divination and fortune telling, self-medication with alcohol and/or drugs (both legal and illegal street drugs), and going to the witch doctor. These activities open us to satan because we are seeking knowledge from the powers of darkness and not trusting Father God about our lives and our future.

If we opened any of these four doors of legal attack by satan unknowingly or even knowingly when we were in the world before we received Jesus into our lives, we need to close these doors, otherwise satan has legal access to continue to trip us up and harass us as we try to walk out our new lives with Jesus. Father God cares about our new lives in Christ and has shared this prayer that will close the four doors of legal harassment by satan:

Heavenly Father, I thank you for your son, Jesus Christ of Nazareth, who went to the cross for me. He is my Lord and Savior!

Jesus, I reject the spirit of fear. I send it straight to the foot of the cross for Jesus Christ of Nazareth to deal with. I refuse to be angry. I reject anger and I send it straight to the foot of the cross for Jesus Christ of Nazareth to deal with. I refuse to participate in sexual promiscuity. I reject the spirit of lust and I send it straight to the foot of the cross for Jesus Christ of Nazareth to deal with. I will only be intimate with my legally wedded spouse or the members of the Godhead. I will not participate in activities of the occult. I reject witchcraft and control and manipulation and I will not seek out the future through divination. I will not go to the witch doctor or drink to excess. I send all of these activities of the occult and witchcraft straight to the foot of the cross for Jesus Christ of Nazareth to deal with. Jesus, I ask that you would close these four doors of legal attack and harassment by satan and seal them shut with your precious blood.

Jesus, I ask that you would sever any unholy or unhealthy soul ties that I may have established and send back to them what belongs to them and bring back to me what belongs to me washed in the precious blood of Jesus.

Jesus, I choose today to forgive anyone who may have ever hurt me, whether they knew it or not. I release them to you and I ask that you would bless them richly with every good gift you have given me and that they would come to know how deeply you love them.

Jesus, if there is any spirit in me that is not of you, I ask that you would take it away right now in Jesus Name. Lord, I ask that you would fill me to overflowing with your

Holy Spirit and that every single part of my heart would be touched by your love and any parts of my mind that were hurt would also be touched by your oil of glory so that I would know that I am yours through and through, in Jesus name I pray.

The Power of our Testimony

The Bible tells us that they overcame by the Blood of the Lamb, the Word of their Testimony and not loving their lives unto death (Revelation 12:11). What does that mean? It means that because Jesus overcame the world and we are His, we have everything we need in order to overcome the world. The Bible tells us that in Him we've been given every divine thing that we need in order to succeed (2 Peter 1:3). We've been given access to the mind of Christ; therefore we have the solutions of Heaven! Jesus tells us that because the world hated Him and we are no longer of this world once we belong to Him, the world is going to hate us too (John 15:18-19). We need to just get over it. We need to actually look on the world hating us as a great blessing because it lets us know that we are on the right track. We are headed towards Victory! Jesus overcame everything and then gave that Victory to us in John 17; if only we would walk in Victory, knowing that we are His. After all, we get to read the end of the book and we know how it ends. We know we've been given everything we need in Jesus and therefore we are overcomers also. The question then becomes, what is the Word of Our Testimony? What is the evidence of Jesus in our lives? What is changing in our lives that we ourselves could not change on our own? How can we demonstrate to the world the ultimate importance of having Jesus in our lives? What is it that Father God wants to show the world through our lives? I believe Father God wants to show the world His plan to help us all become who it is He always made us to be and who it is that He's had faith that we would become. Even when the world gives up on us, Father God never does! Probably because His Son, Jesus, paid such a high price for our success!

Once we reconcile ourselves to the fact that the world is not going to like us, then we are able to move on to some of the greatest opportunities ever! We are able to allow Father God to use us to open the eyes of the blind. We're able to allow Father God to use us, those thought of as foolish, to confound those who think themselves to be wise. Over the course of the past year, Father God has been opening my eyes more and more to understanding that statement on a whole new level. I'm now understanding that He is using the foolish me (who I know I am today) and who I now know has little understanding of Kingdom ways or the thoughts of God, to confound my wise self, as I always thought I had things pretty much figured out! Only Father God has a sense of humor like that! I love His humor, don't you? All of Heaven echoes with the rumblings of the laughter coming forth from the Throne Room! The bottom line is, I figure if I can get God to have a good laugh then I'm doing something right. In reality though, I believe Him when He tells me in the Bible that He rejoices over me. I don't need to earn His rejoicing over me - that's just who He is!

The Transformation of Zacchaeus

What about Zacchaeus (Luke 19:2-9)? What did it look like when Jesus ministered to Zacchaeus?

Zacchaeus was a tax collector. He was apparently a short man whom we don't know a lot about. What we can see in scripture is that this man had heard about a man named Jesus and he wanted to at least see who He was. When we take the time to talk with God as we read the scriptures, we can see the scriptures unfold before our eyes and we can learn from this story in our lives today.

Zacchaeus was a short man who most likely struggled all his life with being teased. In our own lives we can see people like that who get pushed aside all the time until they start to feel unworthy and sometimes rise up with an angry spirit that is not Godly. What if Zacchaeus was smart, but because of being short no one ever saw his greatness? You would think a tax collector would need to have some intelligence and education. The Bible tells us Zacchaeus was thought of as a sinner by the rest of the people in the area. He was also known to be rich in an area where most people didn't have wealth. He was doing well in his career and was in a position over others as the Chief Tax Collector. He was most likely very knowledgeable and knew how to get the money people owed in taxes. A person like this probably hurt a lot of people along the way, right or wrong. No matter who this man was, apparently, he was hungry for something more in his life. He was hungry to know Jesus. He wanted to meet Him or to at least lock eyes on Him as He walked down the street.

Zacchaeus had a passion to overcome every obstacle in his way to see who this Jesus was. He was willing to go out on a tree limb to get up above everyone else to be in a better position to see.

As Zacchaeus climbed up that tree, I believe that his hunger pulled on heaven. What if in that moment, God saw the hunger in Zacchaeus creating an atmosphere shift that caused heaven and earth meet. In that moment, time stood still just for one man who the world did not value. God saw this amazing son who was hungry for something more in his life and He highlighted him to Jesus. We can look at our own lives and see moments like this where heaven moved, and earth stood still for us until the Lord fully encountered us in an answer to our hunger.

What are you hungry for in life? Will your hunger cause heaven to come into your life to change the very atmosphere where you stand?

I believe Father God highlighted Zacchaeus to Jesus, showing the importance of our relationship with God the Father. What if in the moment when Jesus locked eyes on Zacchaeus, the Father revealed to Jesus everything he needed to know about Zacchaeus? When Jesus saw Zacchaeus, time stopped, and the direction Jesus was heading was shifted and directed towards one man. The day Jesus was heading to Jerusalem to go to the cross Jesus stops for one more person. Can you imagine being that person and what it might have felt like to walk in the shoes of Zacchaeus all of his life? Can you imagine being Zacchaeus in that tree, locking eyes on Jesus after going out on the limb of life to know who Jesus really was? My heart races just thinking of that moment! Can you imagine that moment when Jesus' path changed, and He headed towards Zacchaeus in that tree? What grabs my attention is that Jesus knew Zacchaeus' name and wanted to go to his house to eat. Did the Father reveal his name to Jesus? I don't believe Jesus knew everyone's name but scripture says that Jesus only spoke what the Father spoke.

Can you imagine Jesus as a man, standing before you wanting to go to your house to eat with you? In that moment, Jesus shut the mouth of the enemy, silencing his accusations and also shut the mouths of all those who were mummering and complaining about who Zacchaeus was. In that moment Jesus also became the door that opened the heart of the Father to embrace Zacchaeus for the first time in his life. Jesus is the only way to the Father. I believe that through His relationship with the Father, Jesus knew who was pulling on the heart strings of the Father. I believe Jesus used the prophetic to truly know who Zacchaeus was and chose to speak life into him. Jesus had access to the compassionate heart of the Father in which it allowed Him to unlock the pain in Zacchaeus heart. I believe in that moment, a lifetime of pain left Zacchaeus and God the Father touched His son, Zacchaeus, for the first time revealing the Love of the Father.

In that one moment, Jesus saw a sinner who was hated by people turned into a man full of love. It takes a lot of love to be willing to give half of everything you own to the poor and to also give back 4 times the amount of money to anyone you wronged.

What a transformation! It truly was an encounter with the one true living God, Jesus Christ. We also have those opportunities when we have a relationship with Jesus, God the Father, and the Holy Spirit and we can also see the "Zacchaeus" in our life transformed in a heartbeat.

How to reverse the plans of the enemy?

John 10:10 is a valuable scripture, but how often do we allow the battle to overtake us? How can we battle the enemy?

John 10:10. "The thief comes only to steal, kill, and destroy, I have come that they may have life, and have it to the full."

Jesus reveals that he is the good shepherd in John 10:14. He knows his sheep and they know him also. We will know his voice. As we learn to spend time with Lord, we learn to hear his voice clearer. When we hear any other voice we will recognize it is not the Lord's voice and we can cast those thoughts down.

Scripture also says, "Do not conformed to the pattern of the world, but to be transformed by the renewing of your mind. Then you will be able to test and approve what God's will is – his good, pleasing and perfect will." Romans 12:2.

One way to do this is through a tool that helps you to identify the lies you have been believing.

Did you know that we become what we think? When we believe a lie, it starts to become a part of our thinking process. We are to take our thoughts captive and cast them down. In Proverbs 23:7, "As a man thinks in his heart, so is he." How do we cast these thoughts down? As we recognize the lies of the enemy, we acknowledge we need to repent for believing the lie and hand it over to Jesus. We then invite the Holy Spirit into that place where we believed the lie. The Holy Spirit is the key to help remove the pain and trauma attached to that lie. Holy Spirit can reveal revelation to us as we start our healing process. Then we can ask the Father to replace the lie with truth. As you meditate on the truth God reveals to you, you will start to see the revelation of the Fathers love wash over us and the truth will start to come alive inside of us and our foundation within us will start to be healed.

I = Identify the Lie

C = Confess the Lie to Jesus

H = Hand over the lie to Jesus

I = Invite the Holy Spirit into that area of woundedness

M = Ask the Father for Truth to replace the Lie. Then Make a kingdom declaration so you can meditate on the Truth

Redefining a fact you have been believing all your life

Most of us have been building our lives on faulty foundations. Yes, most of us have believed lies about ourselves since we have been in our mother's womb.

Let's practice allowing the Holy Spirit to reveal some lies you are believing. As the Holy Spirit starts to reveal the lies, we can practice the "5 Step Wholeness Steps" by Katie Mather is highly recommended

References

References are taken from the Bible (NKJV, KJV, NIV, ESV, The Passion Translation)

References are taken from "Radical Christianity 101" by Edith Houghton and Trina Olson

References are taken from "5 Step Wholeness Steps" by Katie Mather

Books to Check out:

"The Practice of the Presence of God" by Brother Lawrence

"5 Step Wholeness Steps" by Katie Mather

"Radical Christianity 101" by Edith Houghton and Trina Olson

Cover Design by Trina Olson

Edited by Tina Hoover and Katie Clampit

Empowering a Generation to have a voice

Unleashed publishing is opening doors to empower others to see their gifts and talents come alive. We feel the Author usually has a great story but without the right cover or illustrations, it is just another book. The cover is the first thing that gets someone's attention. The editor brings the book alive and with the convergence of the three you have a book that will leap off the shelf because it will satisfy the reader from cover to cover.

Trina Olson and Edith Houghton with Unleashed Publishing, Inc. maybe contacted through email: trinaolson@radicallaunch.org or Radicallaunch@gmail.com

Unleashed Publishing, Inc.
Unleashing the potential authors, editors, and illustrators of a generation.